Interior Design Mood Board and Imagery Collection Journal

An Interior Designer's Organizing Book Journal and Portfolio of Projects

VIRGINIA I SMITH

D1609363

Copyright © 2020 Virginia I Smith. All rights reserved.

Images used and modified under license - by 123rf.com

Thank you for your purchase

We hope you enjoy using this book. If there is anything you feel may be great to add (or remove), please don't hesitate to leave a comment or a review. Shop our other interior design, project management, and interior architecture related workbooks, activity books, sketchbooks, journals, logbooks, and business books created specifically for interior designers, interior architects, project managers, furniture designers, and teachers and students of art and design studies at:

https://www.amazon.com/-/e/B07ZPHJD8R

INDUSTRY-RELATED BOOKS

ASIN: B0BF2XBCMG

ASIN: B0B7Q3DXFW

ASIN: B092H9V4YG

ASIN: B0BJNBVK35

ASIN: B08PQRSVTG

ASIN: B08KH3R53Q

Interior Design Student
PORTFOLIO AND IMAGERY JOURNAL

ASIN: B08BRKDYTV

ASIN: B09RG5MC5V

ASIN: B09W46FJGW

ASIN: B0955KBJ7N

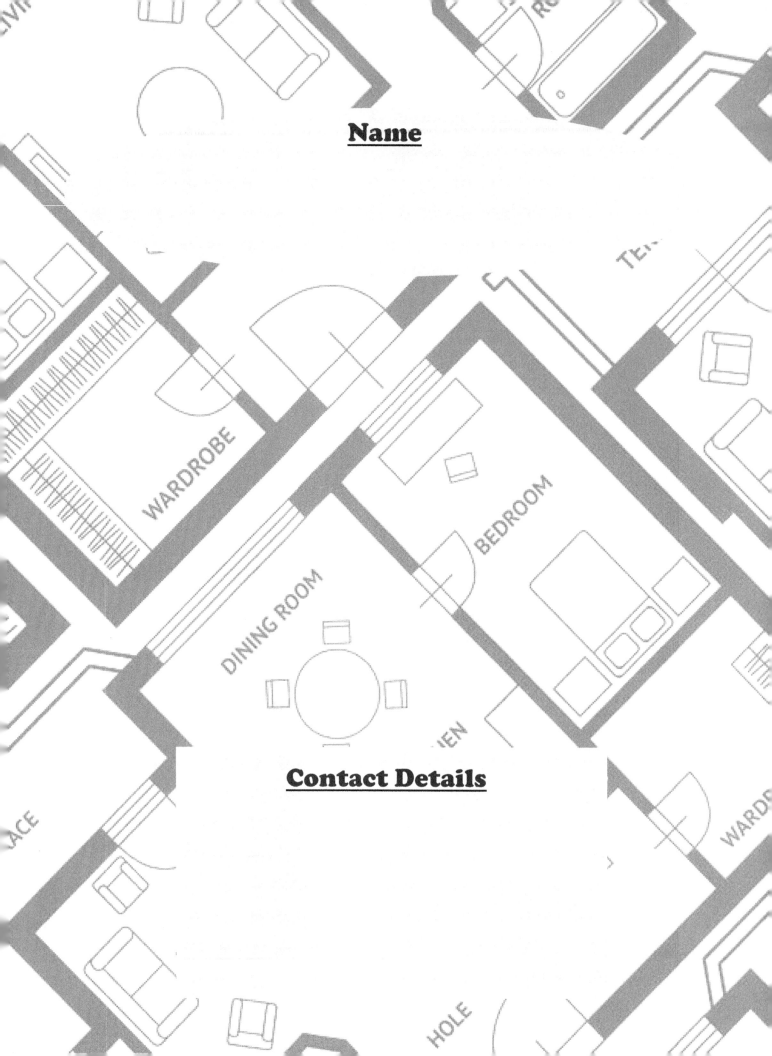

Name

Contact Details

MY INTRODUCTION

Tasks

☐ ....
☐ ....
☐ ....
☐ ....
☐ ....
☐ ....
☐ ....
☐ ....
☐ ....
☐ ....
☐ ....
☐ ....
☐ ....
☐ ....
☐ ....
☐ ....
☐ ....
☐ ....
☐ ....
☐ ....
☐ ....
☐ ....
☐ ....

☐ ....
☐ ....
☐ ....
☐ ....
☐ ....
☐ ....
☐ ....
☐ ....
☐ ....
☐ ....
☐ ....
☐ ....
☐ ....
☐ ....
☐ ....
☐ ....
☐ ....
☐ ....
☐ ....
☐ ....
☐ ....
☐ ....
☐ ....

Duties

Plans

Project/Assignment

Code/# [   ]   Date [   ]

Title [   ]

Location [   ]

Room/Space [   ]   Size [   ]   Area [   ]   Status [   ]

Theme/Style [   ]   Scheme [   ]

Other Details

Brief

_____
_____
_____
_____
_____
_____
_____
_____
_____
_____
_____
_____
_____
_____

Objective

_____
_____
_____
_____
_____
_____
_____
_____
_____
_____
_____
_____
_____
_____

Notes #1

_____

_____

_____

_____

_____

_____

_____

_____

Notes #2

_____

_____

_____

_____

_____

_____

_____

_____

Notes #3

_____

_____

_____

_____

_____

_____

_____

_____

Notes #4

_____

_____

_____

_____

_____

_____

_____

_____

Mood
Pages

Color Scheme

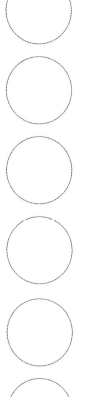

Notes

Notes

Notes

Imagery Collection

Notes

Concluding
Notes

Product Names

Supplier Details

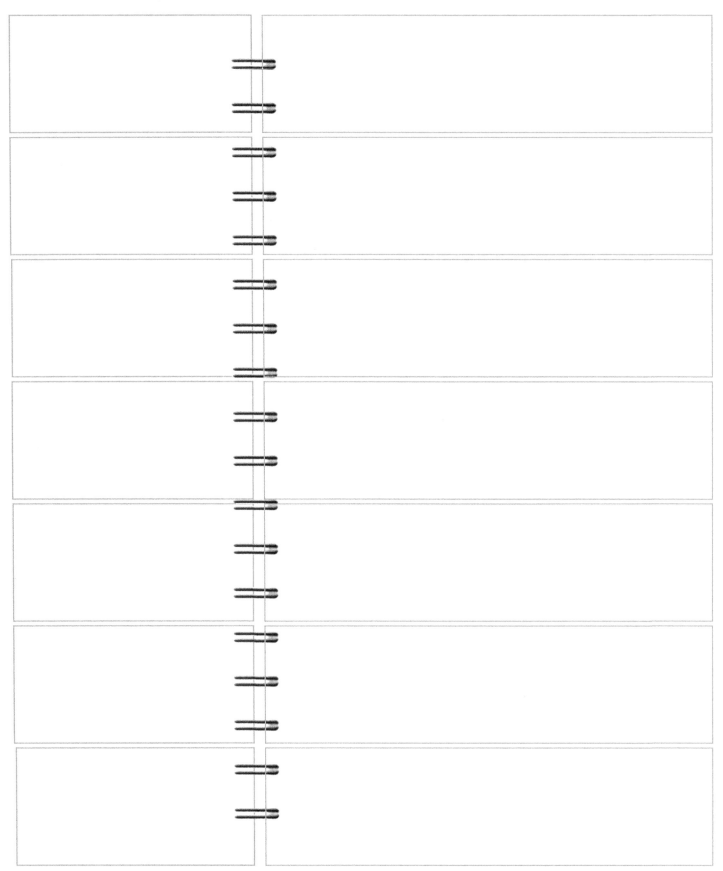

Product Names

Supplier Details

Quick-Sketches

<u>**Description/Notes**</u>

Project/Assignment

Code/# [   ]   Date [   ]

Title [   ]

Location [   ]

Room/Space [   ]   Size [   ]   Area [   ]   Status [   ]

Theme/Style [   ]   Scheme [   ]

Other Details

[   ] [   ] [   ] [   ] [   ]

Brief   **Objective**

_____   _____
_____   _____
_____   _____
_____   _____
_____   _____
_____   _____
_____   _____
_____   _____
_____   _____
_____   _____
_____   _____
_____   _____
_____   _____
_____   _____
_____   _____
_____   _____

Notes #1

Notes #2

Notes #3

Notes #4

Mood Pages

Color Scheme

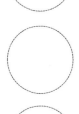

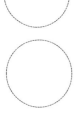

Notes

Notes

Notes

Imagery Collection

<u>Notes</u>

Concluding Notes

Product Names

Supplier Details

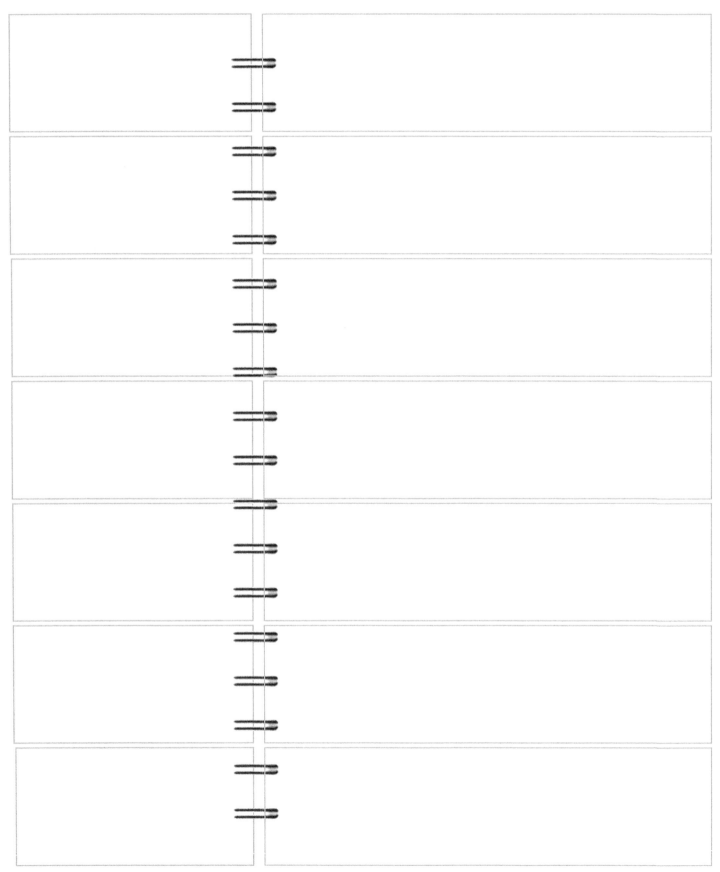

Product Names

Supplier Details

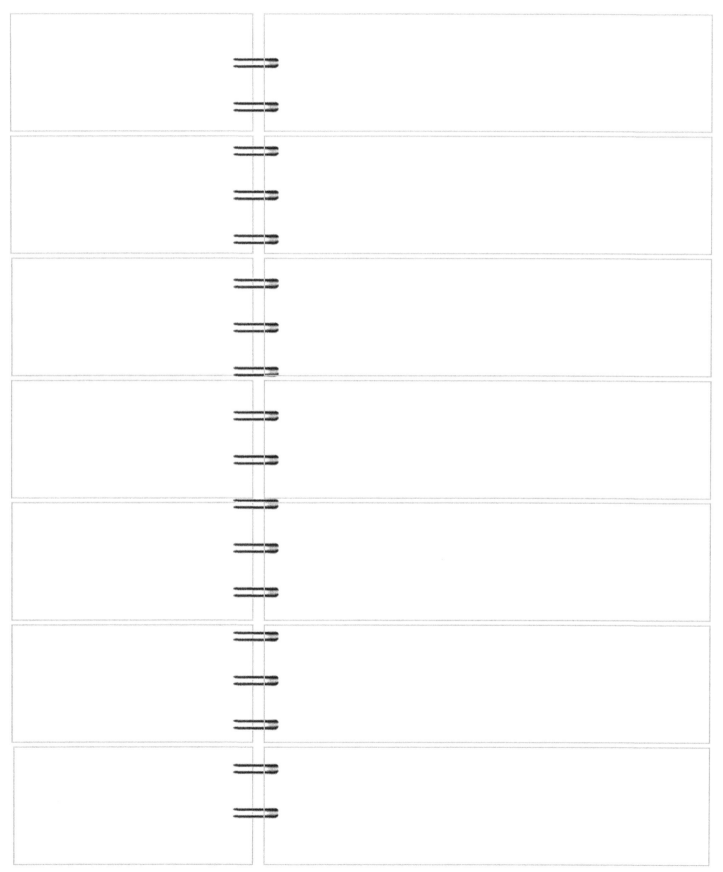

Quick-Sketches

Description/Notes

Project/Assignment

Code/#　[　　　]　　　　　　　　　　　Date　[　　　　　]

Title　[　　　　　　　　　　　　　　　　　　　　　]

Location　[　　　　　　　　　　　　　　　　　　　]

Room/Space　[　　　]　　Size　[　　　]　　Area　[　　　]　　Status　[　　　]

Theme/Style　[　　　　　　　]　　Scheme　[　　　　　]

Other Details

Brief

_____
_____
_____
_____
_____
_____
_____
_____
_____
_____
_____
_____
_____
_____
_____

Objective

_____
_____
_____
_____
_____
_____
_____
_____
_____
_____
_____
_____
_____
_____
_____

Notes #1

Notes #2

Notes #3

Notes #4

Mood
Pages

Color Scheme

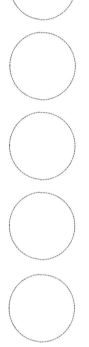

Notes

Notes

Notes

Imagery Collection

Notes

Concluding
Notes

Product Names

Supplier Details

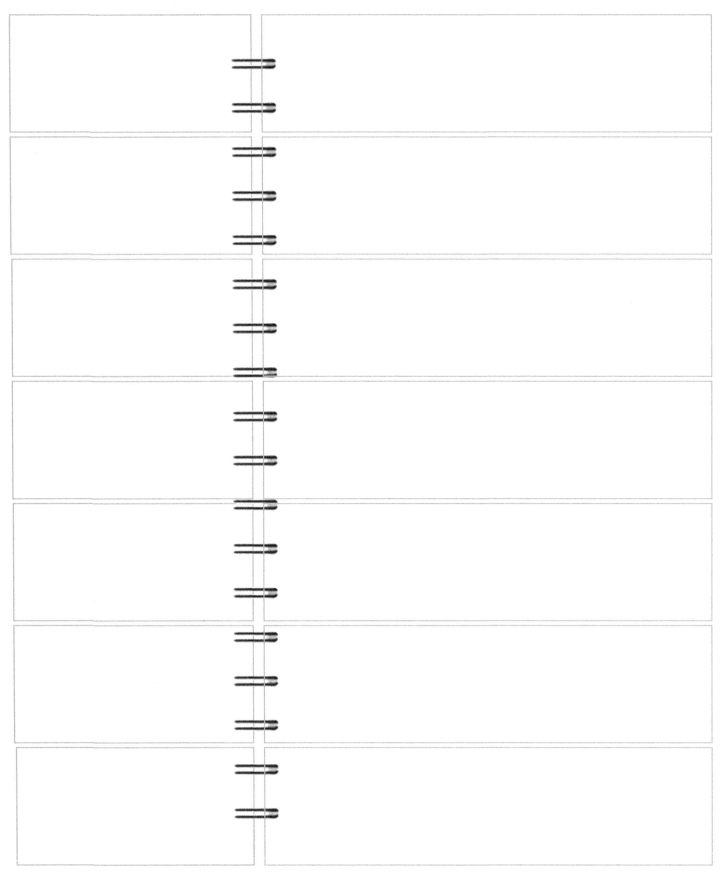

Product Names

Supplier Details

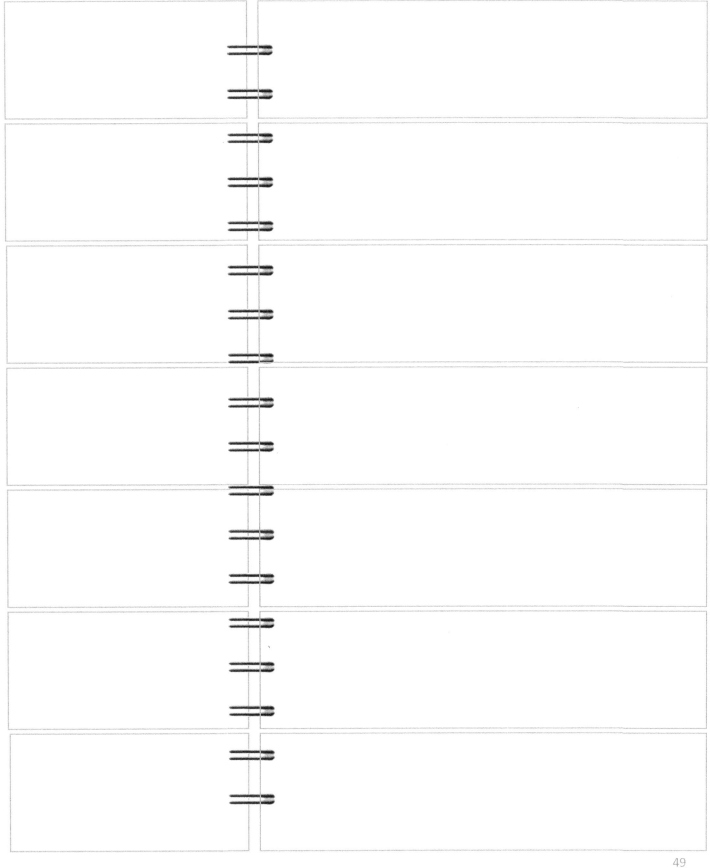

Quick-Sketches

Description/Notes

Project/Assignment

Code/# [   ]   Date [   ]

Title [   ]

Location [   ]

Room/Space [   ]   Size [   ]   Area [   ]   Status [   ]

Theme/Style [   ]   Scheme [   ]

Other Details

Brief

_____
_____
_____
_____
_____
_____
_____
_____
_____
_____
_____
_____
_____
_____
_____
_____

Objective

_____
_____
_____
_____
_____
_____
_____
_____
_____
_____
_____
_____
_____
_____
_____
_____

Notes #1

Notes #2

Notes #3

Notes #4

Mood
Pages

Color Scheme

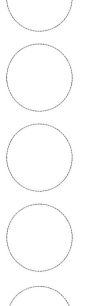

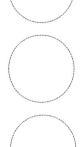

Notes

Swatches & Samples

Notes

Notes

Imagery Collection

<u>Notes</u>

Concluding Notes

Product Names

Supplier Details

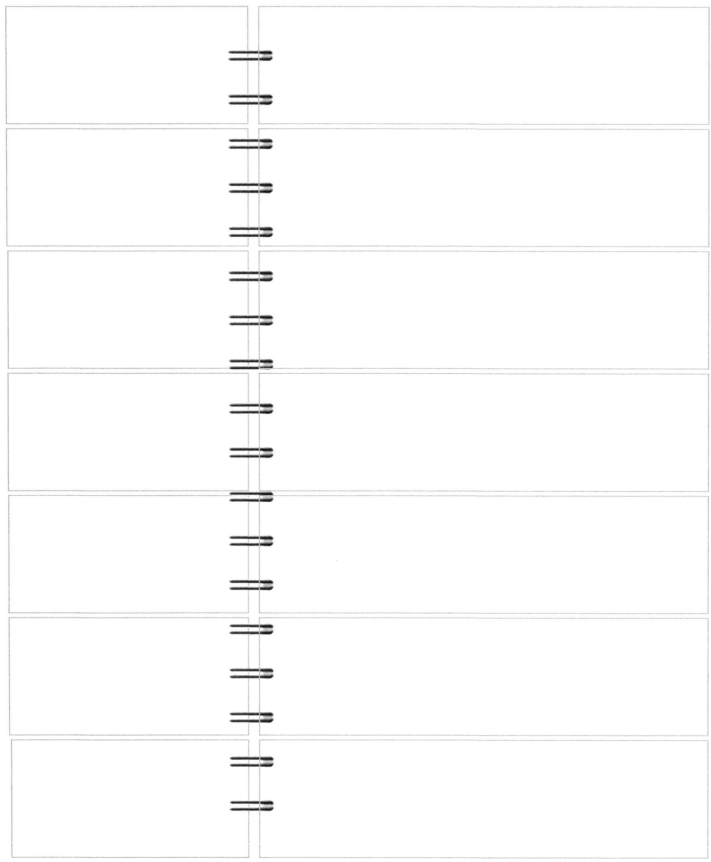

Product Names

Supplier Details

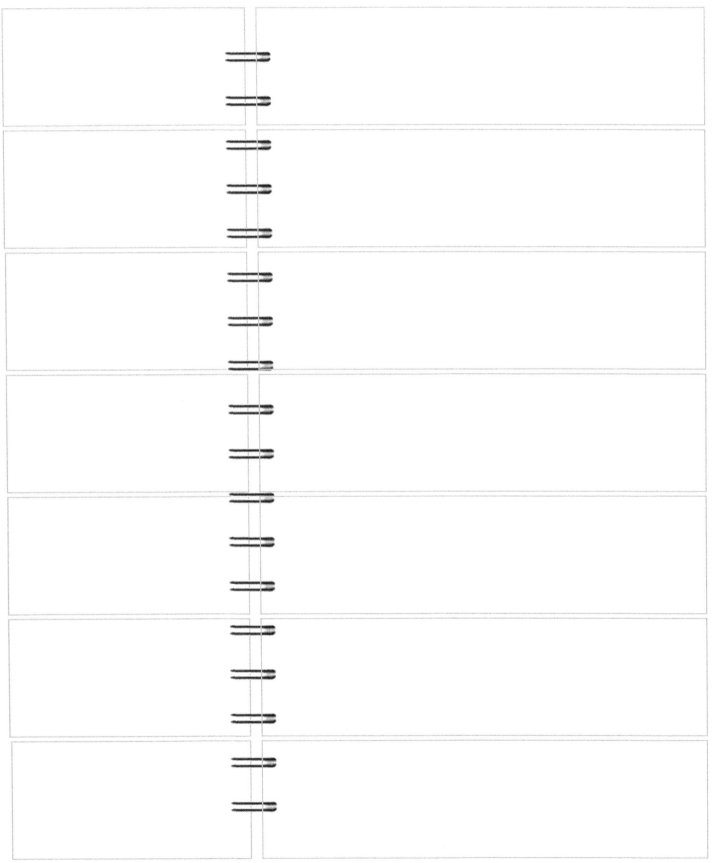

Quick-Sketches

Description/Notes

Project/Assignment

Code/# [   ]   Date [   ]

Title [   ]

Location [   ]

Room/Space [   ]   Size [   ]   Area [   ]   Status [   ]

Theme/Style [   ]   Scheme [   ]

Other Details

Brief   ## Objective

_____   _____
_____   _____
_____   _____
_____   _____
_____   _____
_____   _____
_____   _____
_____   _____
_____   _____
_____   _____
_____   _____
_____   _____
_____   _____
_____   _____
_____   _____
_____   _____
_____   _____

Notes #1

Notes #2

Notes #3

Notes #4

Mood Pages

Color Scheme

Notes

Notes

Notes

Imagery Collection

Notes

Concluding Notes

Product Names

Supplier Details

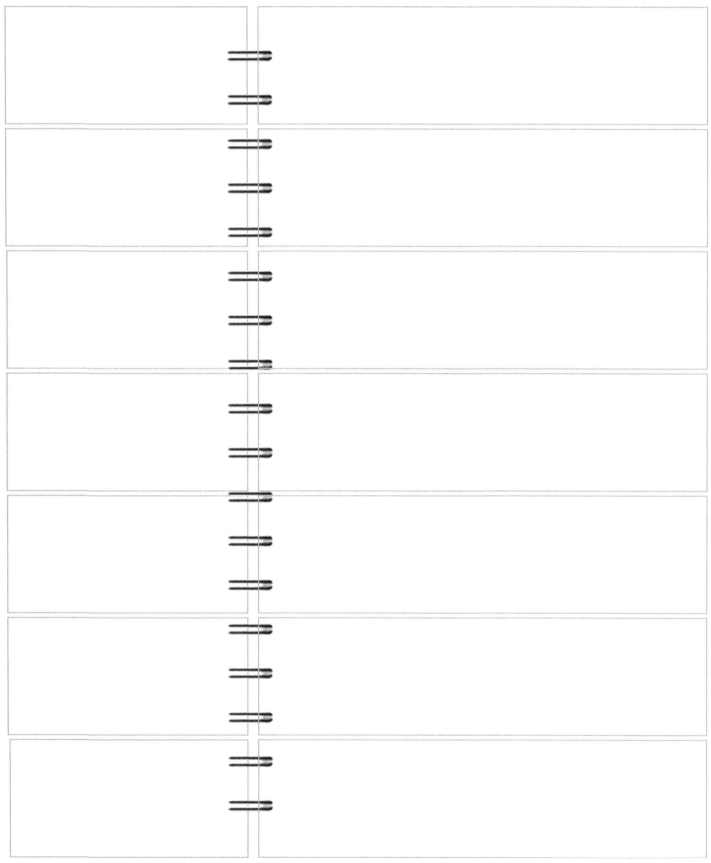

Product Names

Supplier Details

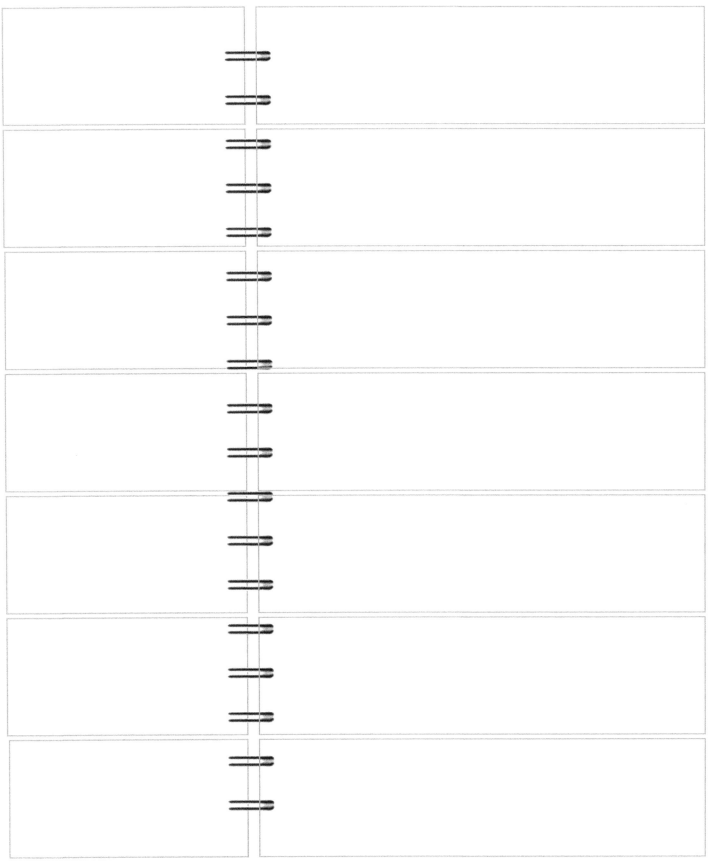

Quick-Sketches

Description/Notes

Project/Assignment

Code/# [   ]   Date [   ]

Title [   ]

Location [   ]

Room/Space [   ]   Size [   ]   Area [   ]   Status [   ]

Theme/Style [   ]   Scheme [   ]

Other Details

Brief   **Objective**

_____   _____
_____   _____
_____   _____
_____   _____
_____   _____
_____   _____
_____   _____
_____   _____
_____   _____
_____   _____
_____   _____
_____   _____
_____   _____
_____   _____
_____   _____
_____   _____
_____   _____

Notes #1

Notes #2

Notes #3

Notes #4

Mood
Pages

Color Scheme

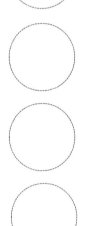

Notes

Swatches & Samples

Notes

Notes

Imagery Collection

Notes

Concluding Notes

Product Names

Supplier Details

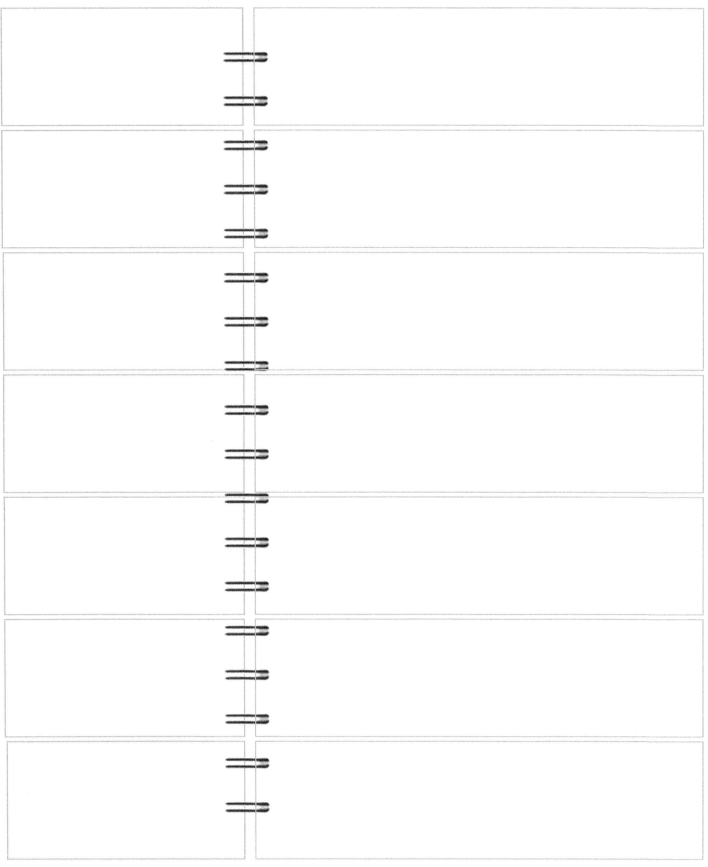

Product Names

Supplier Details

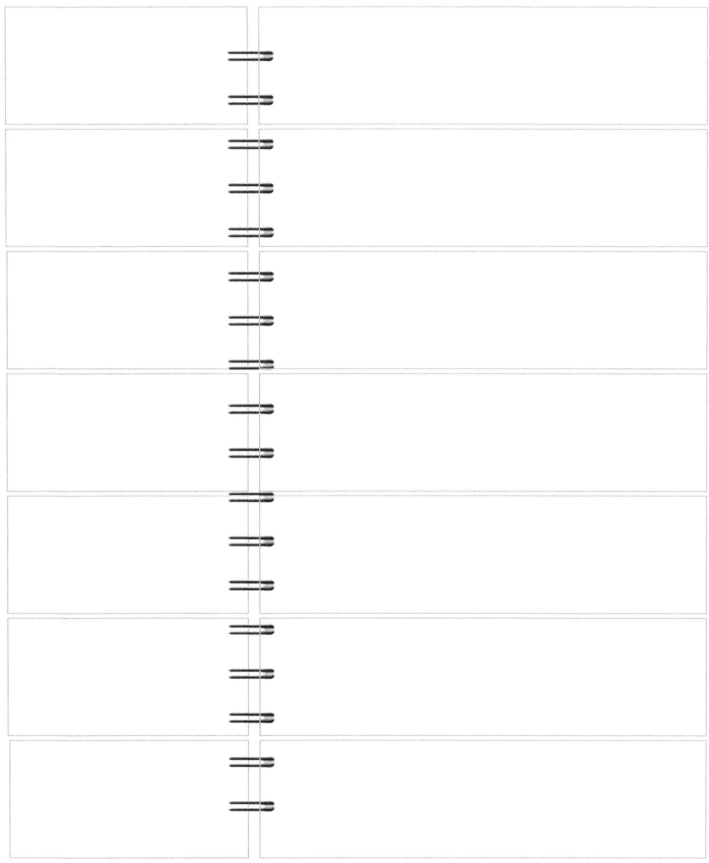

Quick-Sketches

Description/Notes

93

Project/Assignment

Code/# [   ]   Date [   ]

Title [   ]

Location [   ]

Room/Space [   ]   Size [   ]   Area [   ]   Status [   ]

Theme/Style [   ]   Scheme [   ]

Other Details

Brief

_____

Objective

_____

Notes #1

Notes #2

Notes #3

Notes #4

Mood Pages

Color Scheme

Notes

Notes

Notes

Imagery Collection

Notes

Concluding
Notes

Product Names

Supplier Details

Product Names

Supplier Details

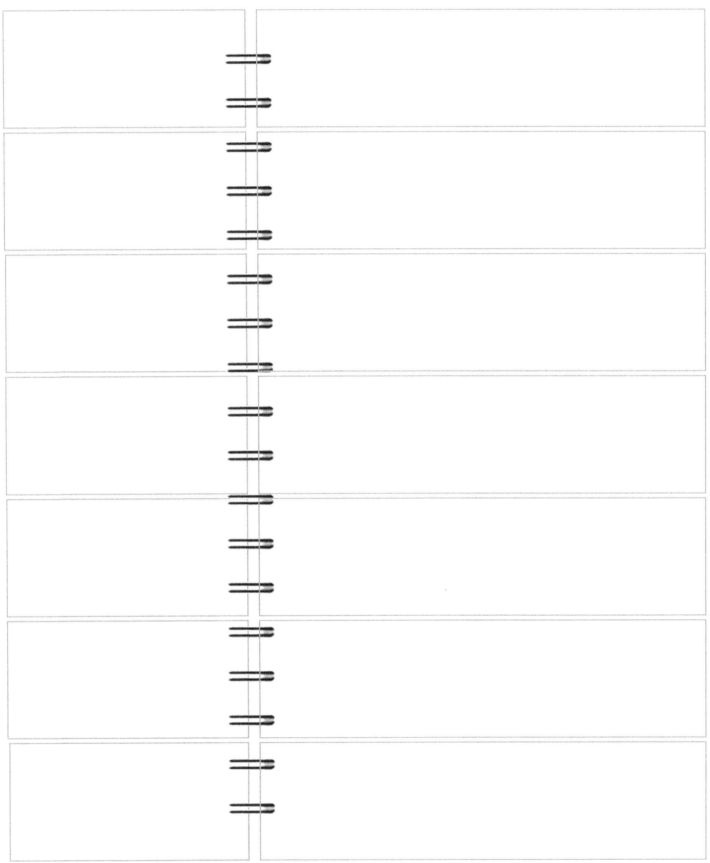

Quick-Sketches

Description/Notes

Project/Assignment

Code/# [ ]   Date [ ]

Title [ ]

Location [ ]

Room/Space [ ]   Size [ ]   Area [ ]   Status [ ]

Theme/Style [ ]   Scheme [ ]

Other Details

Brief   ## Objective

Notes #1

Notes #2

Notes #3

Notes #4

Mood
Pages

Color Scheme

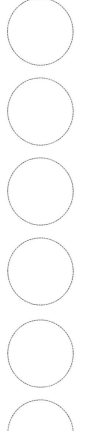

Notes

Notes

Notes

Imagery Collection

Notes

Concluding
Notes

Product Names

Supplier Details

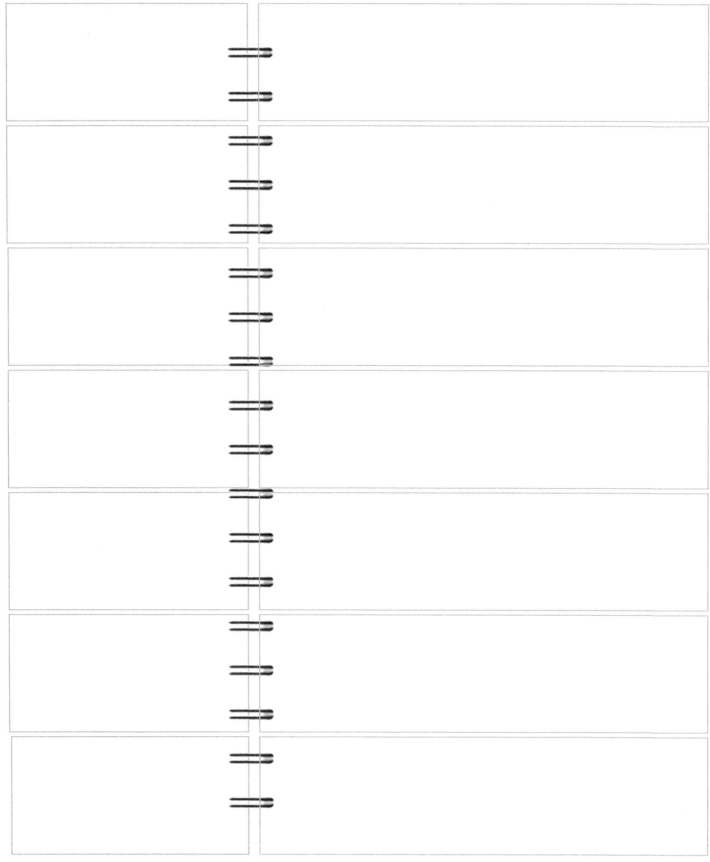

Product Names

Supplier Details

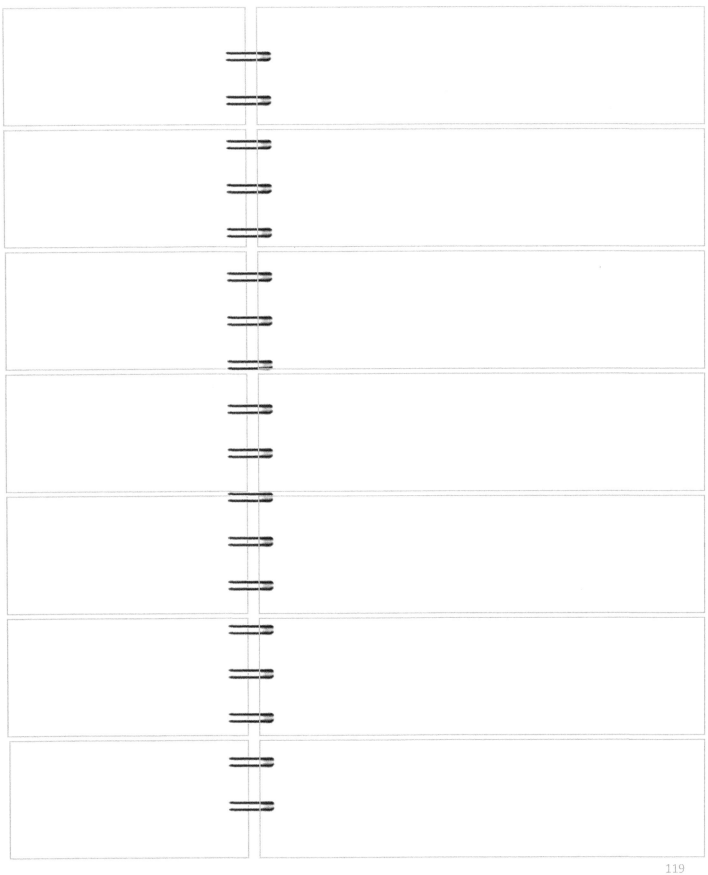

Quick-Sketches

Description/Notes

Project/Assignment

Code/# [   ]   Date [   ]

Title [   ]

Location [   ]

Room/Space [   ]   Size [   ]   Area [   ]   Status [   ]

Theme/Style [   ]   Scheme [   ]

Other Details

[   ] [   ] [   ] [   ] [   ]

Brief   ## Objective

Notes #1

Notes #2

Notes #3

Notes #4

Mood Pages

Color Scheme

Notes

Notes

Notes

Imagery Collection

Notes

Concluding Notes

Product Names

Supplier Details

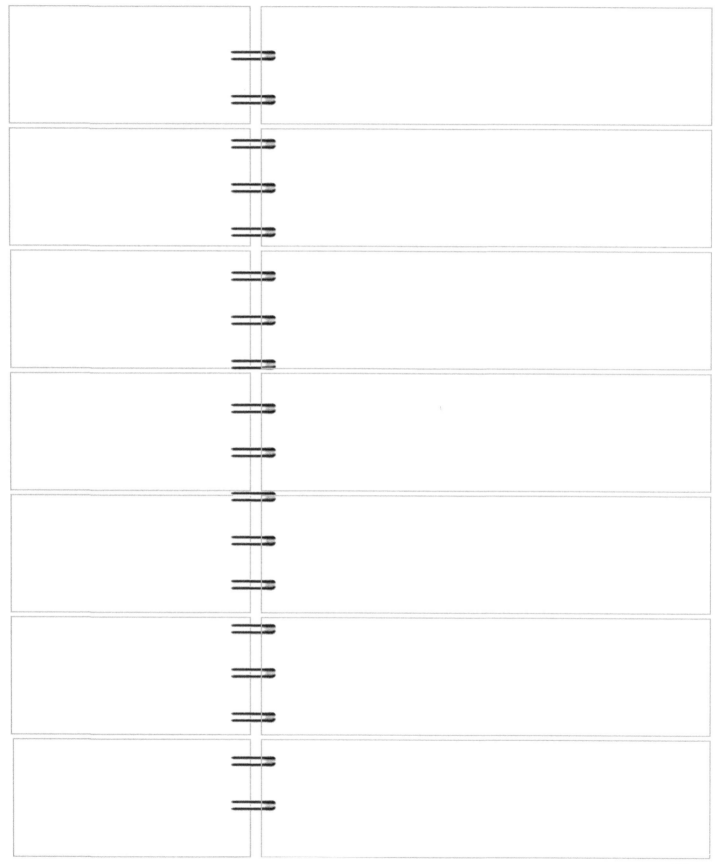

Product Names

Supplier Details

Quick-Sketches

Description/Notes

Project/Assignment

Code/# [   ]   Date [   ]

Title [   ]

Location [   ]

Room/Space [   ]   Size [   ]   Area [   ]   Status [   ]

Theme/Style [   ]   Scheme [   ]

Other Details

Brief   ## Objective

Notes #1

Notes #2

Notes #3

Notes #4

Mood Pages

Color Scheme

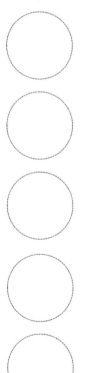

Notes

Notes

Notes

Imagery Collection

Notes

Concluding
Notes

Product Names

Supplier Details

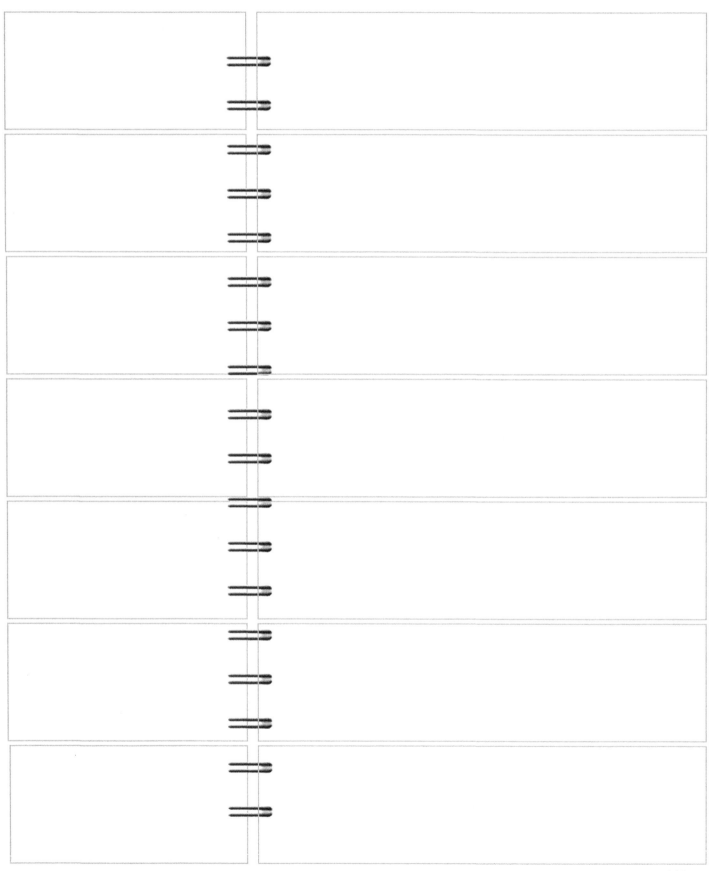

Product Names

Supplier Details

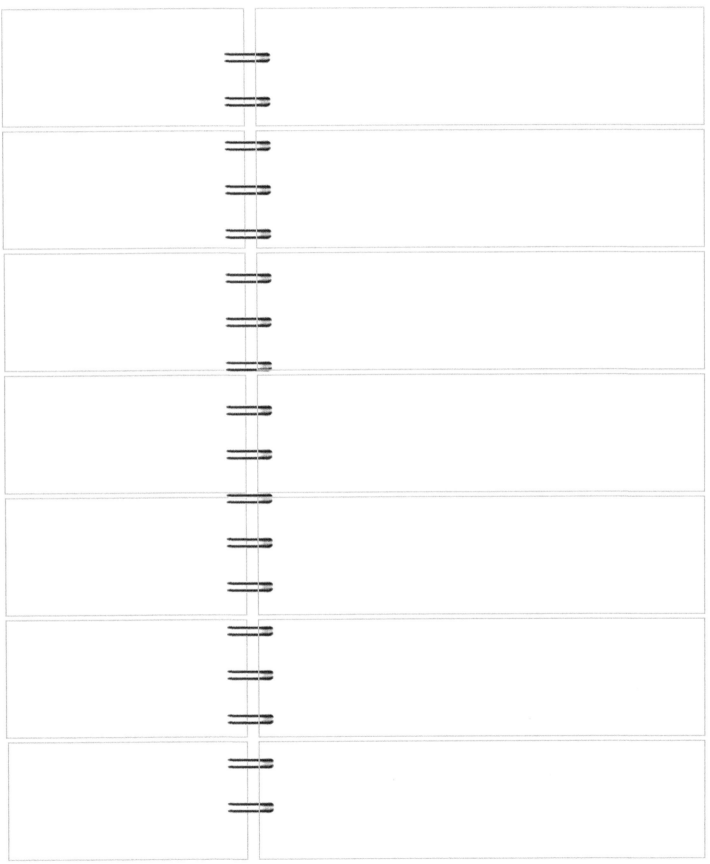

Quick-Sketches

Description/Notes

Project/Assignment

Code/# [   ]   Date [   ]

Title [   ]

Location [   ]

Room/Space [   ]   Size [   ]   Area [   ]   Status [   ]

Theme/Style [   ]   Scheme [   ]

Other Details

Brief   ## Objective

_____   _____
_____   _____
_____   _____
_____   _____
_____   _____
_____   _____
_____   _____
_____   _____
_____   _____
_____   _____
_____   _____
_____   _____
_____   _____
_____   _____
_____   _____
_____   _____

Notes #1

Notes #2

Notes #3

Notes #4

Mood Pages

<u>Color Scheme</u>

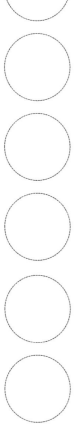

Notes

Notes

Notes

Imagery Collection

Notes

Concluding Notes

Product Names

Supplier Details

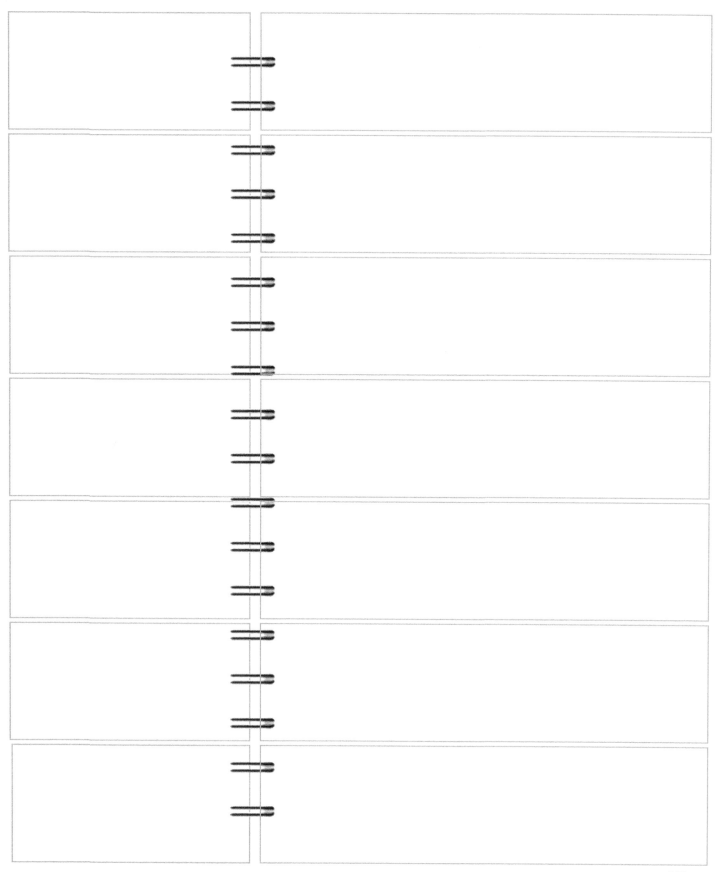

Product Names

Supplier Details

Quick-Sketches

Description/Notes

Project/Assignment

Code/# [_____]   Date [_____]

Title [_____]

Location [_____]

Room/Space [_____]   Size [_____]   Area [_____]   Status [_____]

Theme/Style [_____]   Scheme [_____]

Other Details

[_____] [_____] [_____] [_____] [_____]

Brief   **Objective**

_____   _____
_____   _____
_____   _____
_____   _____
_____   _____
_____   _____
_____   _____
_____   _____
_____   _____
_____   _____
_____   _____
_____   _____
_____   _____
_____   _____
_____   _____
_____   _____
_____   _____
_____   _____

Notes #1

Notes #2

Notes #3

Notes #4

Mood Pages

Color Scheme

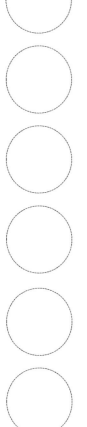

Notes

Notes

Notes

Imagery Collection

<u>Notes</u>

Concluding
Notes

Product Names

Supplier Details

Product Names

Supplier Details

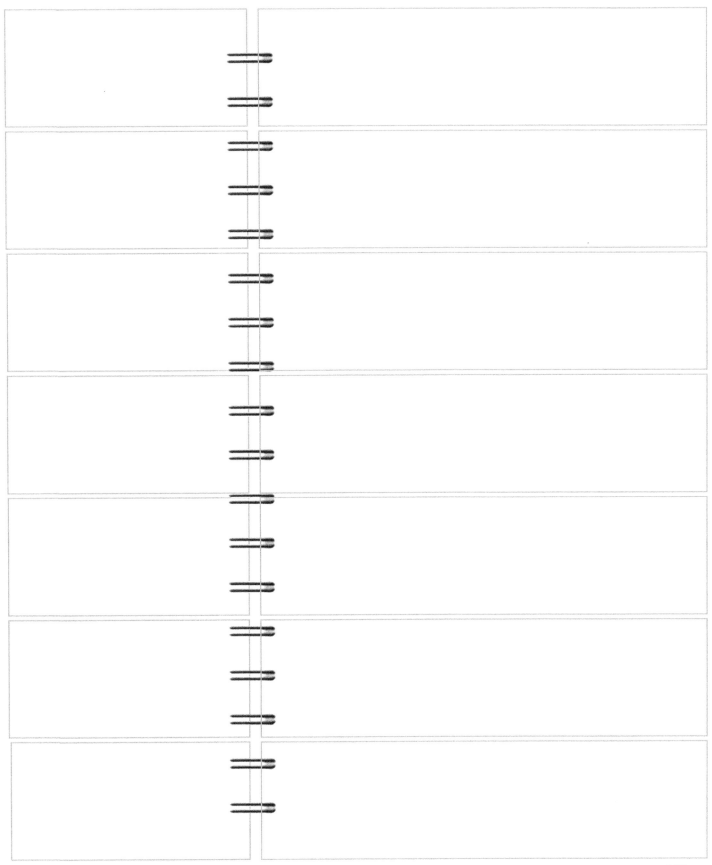

Quick-Sketches

Description/Notes

Index

DATE	TOPIC	PAGE

Index

DATE	TOPIC	PAGE

Index

DATE	TOPIC	PAGE

Index

DATE	TOPIC	PAGE

31461947R00104